TATTOO
LAND

TATTOO LAND

Kathleen McCracken

Exile Editions

Publishers of singular
Fiction, Poetry, Translation, Drama, Nonfiction and Graphic Books

2009

Design and Composition by KellEnK Styleset
Cover/Interior Lithograph by permission of Gabriela Campos
Typeset in Bembo at the Moons of Jupiter Studios
Printed in Canada by Gauvin Imprimerie

The publisher would like to acknowledge the financial assistance
of The Canada Council for the Arts and the Ontario Arts Council.

Published in Canada in 2009 by Exile Editions Ltd.
144483 Southgate Road 14
General Delivery
Holstein, Ontario, N0G 2A0
info@exileeditions.com
www.ExileEditions.com

Canadian Sales Distribution:
McArthur & Company
c/o Harper Collins
1995 Markham Road
Toronto, ON M1B 5M8
toll free: 1 800 387 0117

U.S. Sales Distribution:
Independent Publishers Group
814 North Franklin Street
Chicago, IL 60610
www.ipgbook.com
toll free: 1 800 888 4741

for J
solo amado

So this Green Automobile:
>   I give you in flight
>   a present, a present
>   from my imagination.

—ALLEN GINSBERG, "The Green Automobile"

Footprints runnin' 'cross the silver sand
Steps goin' down into tattoo land
I met the sons of darkness and the sons of light
In the bordertowns of despair

—BOB DYLAN, "Dignity"

Contents

III

IV

I

Snow Tea

for Robert and Shirley McCracken

That June the lilacs came in heavy
as if they knew something about the summer in store.
Fiesta, we called them, manna from the western mountains.
(I was ten, he was thirty seven)
With a bone hilted Texas jackknife
he cut their corded stems
through milkweed pastures carried them
armfuls of raincloud, back to me counting
nickels in his flatbed pickup truck.

༄

A butcher by default, he was
mad about motors, tinkering in the shop
or on the lawn – outboards, mowers, dirt bikes, pumps.
I'd bring us Cokes and sing the choruses from *Blonde on Blonde*
(I was fifteen, he was forty two)
and he'd say fetch that ratchet, I want to show you
how to drain this oil tank down.

༄

They were married on a Monday in Toronto
the third of June, nineteen and fifty seven
Buddy Holly on the radio singing *That'll be the day*
the world before John Glenn and LuAnn Simms.

He drove a two tone customized Ford Fairlane
my mother wore French lipstick, candy apple red
trim bodice, knee length skirt, stiletto heels
edged with rhinestone glances.

The rest is mostly mystery, arcane
terrain belonging exclusively to them
but when they made the golden fifty mark
(yellow rose in his lapel, Japhet orchid at her wrist) ·

I wrote to say how sure I was
I'd caught a glimpse of that same car
its chrome tipped fins and ice cone tail lights
clocking sixty on the road to Boshkung Lake
and in its wake a show of swimming kites
cut from just above the whitest gem set hem.

ॐ

I can scarcely see my father now, his face I mean.
You know he had a tattoo, left bicep, from the war.
Good thing, I guess, she kept those photos of him.
Mac his buddies called him, he was always camera shy.
What do you remember, the first thing?

Suppose it was the ring, your gold wedding band
the one that won't come off for love nor money, so you say.
That and the fireworks.
It must have been the twenty fourth of May, Victoria Day

you were pushing me sky high on a swing
and in the black beyond a palamino mare
one hoof raised, over by Jake Hill's dammed up pond.

Yeah I remember that time too
it was well before the lakehouse, you were small.
No one was taking pictures, it was after dark
or if there were any they'd be gone by now
what with the couple moves, and then the fire, and all.

❧

There were winters we slept under coats
the three of us, our sisters just the same
in their bedroom up the stairs.
The house as cold as starblown skies.

There were others I split five full cord of maple
stocked the shed up to the rafters, primed
a brand new Franklin stove to heat a home
not Mac nor Florrie in their most dramatic
flights could have dreamed up.

❧

The locals gave good trade, dealt in grain fed
cattle, sheep and swine. Sometimes after hours
brought in out of season game.
I flanked him where he bled and boned
the quartered beeves, the severed sows

learned to churn a cast iron sausage grinder
slice cold cuts, set rumps and briskets in neat rows.
No pollen here, no cornmeal. Instead the rituals
of scrubbing down the wooden block
sprinkling fresh dried sawdust on the floor
in which I read his silence
as the blessing that it was.

❧

Don't, won't, can't. Swim.
Like it fine here in the shade. DuMauriers. Labatts.
You go on I'll watch, you're the fish.
Just be careful not to go on out too far.

❧

He taught Chris how to ride a Honda
build bonfires out of driftwood, play baseball
handle chainsaws, woodplanes, enigmatic spirit levels.
The summer he turned sixteen
took him out to Hopeville each night after work
for eight weeks straight until he learned
to drive stick shift and automatic.

Neither of them cared a whit to fish or hunt
instead they'd paddle lean canoes
way up into the marsh mouths
then tell about the weird things thriving
a mile beneath the mottled surface, or in winter

race Skidoos across the frozen lake
egging the ice to crack and take them down.

It was my brother got his bosun's timbre
his *caballero*'s gait, his hands.
I'd hear them talking outside late at night
with torches, thick as thieves my mother'd say
plotting where to strike up camp
at what angle to Polaris fell the dead limbed elm
the one they called the lightning tree.
Every word familiar, at the same time obsolete
lexicon from far above and deep below
the water's shifting table.

❦

Come here and take a look at this
it's my old Harley Davidson kidney belt
good lord it's small, no way that would go around me now.
Why don't you have it, for a lark?

You know I'm not a driver
doubt I'll ever make a car, much less a bike.

Well you could strap it on for kicks some Friday night
that guy you've got would think it looks real fine
or see that teenage daughter of yours there
give it down to her, you never know, she might.

❦

He was expecting snow that day, spent the morning
putting up storm windows, transistor tuned
to CKNX, *Because you're mine, I walk the line*
and *When the Lord made me he made a ramblin' man.*
At noon there was thunder, lightning, sheets of rain.
My mother on Ward C wondering
where on god's green earth he'd taken himself off to.
It was the last Wednesday in October
run up to All Souls', 1960.
By the time the doctor thought to call
the skies had cleared, it was good driving all the way.
He wasn't the first to notice that strawberry
birthmark, crowning crimson tattoo
that would give in so much auburn
tough strands black as his own.

❧

This world's a windlass, no matter
how you winch it it's beyond the best of us
to set the balance right

Same way you can never dodge
what's writ in stone as yours, unless of course
you care to set your mind to try

❧

We flew down to Orlando in a DC8
(I was nine, he was thirty six)

first time either one of us had been on board
a jet airliner, and I noticed how he noticed
the accumulating stress of each
accelerated revolution, the strangeness
of the engines' shock and shudder
then reclined into surveying
cloud contours skirting moonrise or
the lights below at Nashville, Tennessee.

He bought our mother perfume, Chanel No 5
much taken by the novelty of duty free
and made sure my brother
consumed at eight by aeronautical ambition
paid his kid's fare gratis visit
to the low lit neon cockpit.

Midnight on the airfield, it was humid
I was busy scouting palm trees, maybe
calculating mileage to the Gulf
while he stood gazing at the cooling undercarriage
as if it housed some haunted ark
or a future he'd been ten slim years
too young to see.

❧

There's people in this town
would sooner shoot you stone cold dead
as look you in the eye

there's others'll kindly do the driving
or give you what's laid out for Sunday table
if you can show the need is genuine

Remember that, and cultivate a knack
for letting most of what you find just drift
rain water running off a river duck's back

When his mother died it was Marie who made the call.
Twenty seconds on the line and he was dressing
in the blackedged 8 am—
work shirt, work boots, steam pressed overalls.
(I was seven, he was thirty four)
On the radio Nat Raider. Nat Raider
whose secondhand woodpanel stationwagon
its upholstery steeped in cigar smoke, leathers nicked and torn
by case clasps and the claws of music stands
he'd snagged for a song at the auctions out near Varney in the fall.
Thin man in a downpour he left us
under cotton sheets listening to the blues
our mother doing the weeping while he drove
the twelve miles north to Nanny Florrie's parlour.

Sky's a fine name, it'll serve you
no matter the little fella turns out a boy or girl.

I suppose it's just the thought of all that blue…

And then there'll be those sunshot silver jet streams
I'm at liberty to glass come summer sundown
knowing one of them might easily have left
your side of the pond at noon or thereabouts.

❧

In this photo he is laughing, posed
beside a strung up buck he didn't shoot.
Gray and burgundy bomber jacket
front wheel of the Harley cropped
by the frame. He's just turned twenty
and is thinking back to 1941
Pearl Harbor and his brothers who
as he'd cycled home the breaking news
were staked out, one in Holland, one in France.

❧

How far is so far you won't come back again?

I wonder if he wondered that
when I went west, staked a claim
to the Pacific Rim, holed up for a time
on islands at the country's limit
(I was nineteen, he was forty six)
or later headed off for Ireland

saw fit to put the gravitas
of an entire ocean between us.

If he did he never said, just footed bills
for collect calls and round trip flights
at Christmas and the Twelfth
then came for visits tuned to
building shelves, repairing gates
sizing up a situation
he refused to argue in favour or against—

If you want that gypsy cowboy
half as much as I'm inclined to think you do
looks like here is where you're gonna have to stay.

೪೦೪೦

Times were tough, it was a trade
I was lucky Henders took me on.
Here, have some liver, the iron'll do you good.
No offence but I've decided…
(I was sixteen, he was forty three)
None taken. Guess you'll hoe your own row
same way I've hoed mine.

೪೦೪೦

I'll tell you where I'd like to travel, if I had a choice…

Alaska was the fabled land, pristine aquamarine
frontier where only god and the animals
would converse with him in tongues of mercury
and platinum, on snowfields, icefloes, glacial till.

We could fly out west all the way to Juneau
then take a train on up to Anchorage
there'd be a boat and we'd just cruise
the panhandle, the islands they'd be magic
under that all night white midsummer light.

He had the figure of an otter carved
from ivory walrus tusk, small amulet
made by an Aleut sculptor from Unalaska
and I'd see the way he'd look at it sometimes
as if it held a spirit, or the thought of one.

We'll go sometime, your mother and I
I'd like to see the salmon run, take in the Iditarod
or listen to those bowhead whales, their moans and calls
before the Arctic's lost to melt
the way they say is bound to happen next.

❧

It was August when the lakehouse burned
(I was thirteen, he was forty one)
prized property he'd framed and sided
shingled single handed, more or less

appointed so it caught the setting sun and in winter
the Pleiades where they hung behind birch woods.
He thanked the gods we'd made it out alive
then hardwilled ceased to eat or sleep
until he'd drafted blueprints for a second
its beams and lime foundations
twin, identical – refuge, hideout, home from home
where in the lucent lightning flare
only his faintly arrhythmic heart
could measure the angle of incidence.

❧

Could have sworn I was in Korea, not just my bed
and kit but the whole hospital transported.
There were women in the 4 am, talking low then loud
in a language I think I heard once in a movie...

That would be the morphine, it takes the pain
and you with it.

But what about the wound, it was glowing
underneath the bandages, those sixteen staples humming
and on my tongue there was the aftertaste of some slow burn
a fuse rocketing off out into the dark, where the road is.

❧

Each year on his birthday I would make snow tea.
(He might be pushing seventy, I could be forty three)
He would say how there was nothing like it
Roiboish or Assam or in the morning Earl Grey
brewed from the season's final melt.
He prefers cast iron to aluminium any day
and we always drink from kiln fired glazed clay mugs
to hold the heat against the valley's earth cold April mountain air.

II

Snow Moon

Out over the Cave Hill mountain
the last full moon of the year
is going down, aureole a nacre benediction
casting lots, crossing all our lives.

Folded on the palm of my hand
a paper airplane, its shape in jet black silhouette
against the flares, the lit up rifts and hollows
where the lives of others – downed, deserted, flown –
drift and lie low.

Will It Fly?

Who's to say if these slight wings
can bear the weight of so much air

if the engine's primed to peak
the ballast laid in evenly

if the calculations all add up
to something sound?

Guy wires whine like fiddle strings
or cicadas high on heat

the tail piece shimmies—
a girl's kite, a dragonfly

and etched into the fuselage
autobiographies

that rarefied aluminium
a sheet of aerial parchment.

We fly on faith, you'd say
but all I'll ever know for sure

is when the day arrived
– holy gold, annunciation blue –

the wind kept to its cage and I
did not forget to kiss your soul.'

Just the Sky

What is left to us, after the dog fights and the dawn sorties
the rhymed chimeric purple hearts, the perfumed women
saluting our wild, adrenalized flybys

is nothing anyone, not even that blue eyed boy
ace pilot from Krakow, could have crosshaired
the instruments primed yet being what they were.

Out where the grass cracked runway is curtailed by scrub
a trailer camp, used car lots, strip malls whose children
are girls calling to boys in the language of the spared.

Late born, they will not read the score – nocturne, pianissimo –
graffitied on the radio tower's walls, the stairs that barely
take our weight, climbing to shelter under its cupola of stars.

Lit up by crescent moons, the bombers' flight paths would bisect the lough.
In all of this, you ask, the fall out and the chimeless dereliction
what splinter sifted from the ghostbright rubble remains to recognize?

This side the seapark, six palms and the bladed pampas grass.
Over there the bluestone shore, its coal docks inked against the tide.
Blinded, riddled, cleft, I would find you
                              in crosswinds, in the mineral dark.

Airships

i.

Every four minutes the planes set down
at Sydenham.
Their throttled engines
shred your voice
capsize our conversation
sad longing through salt distance
disquisition on the etymology
of the word *ship*.

ii.

Who hewed and rigged
the North Sea's proto *scip*
its hollowed hull and matrix masts
alone on the cutthroat lough?

What manner man exhaled the flame
of his own name into an acetylene future
where bowsprit became cockpit
gunwales the freighted fuselage?

How does the slippage happen?
Green, hooded, the gods draw back
as earth transmutes to air, displays
a stunning alchemy.

Where do you go the thousand
and one days and nights it takes
to build from balsa and ash
the original replica, heart's ache in flight with it?

iii.

Most of them died
before you were born.

Most of them had foreign accents, sound
bodies pledged to women in two countries.

Most of them were gunners
some of them were bomber pilots.

Most of them were not obsessive.
All of them ate, slept, breathed

                              airships.

iv.

By twelve you'd learned to size each type to perfection
sent the first – sexy silver Queen of the Sky –
out over the bay and back home safe.

At twenty two (stunts for kicks, lone flyer)
painted liberty – eight feet of canvas
a vapour trail heading west.

v.

Late one summer you dreamed of Coney Island
direct connection Aldergrove to JFK.

Ineluctable
precession of the equinoxes.

By midday we had all shifted
into a season of absolute transgressions

two towers
two planes.

In the sky parlour above your bed
the scale model squadron

of Spitfires and Stirlings, Hellcats and Marauders
suffered an imperceptible shudder

before the dust resettled
sifted pall

on wings, rudders,
each glassed in gunner's cage.

vi.

Let's talk about the genesis
of the urge to describe
what it means to really be in love
with light, ghosts, borderlands, liftoff
with going to sea in the heft
of mazarine heavens.

At the close of the second day
I watch you fix the final frame at one
sixteenth of a second, document
the way that Mustang bisects
the horizon's uncompromising
parallelogram of forces.

Windfall

Maybe he had a wife, Oswald Mo.
Who would ever know
Canada lying at such distance
from Norway, or so it seemed.
Tenebrific midwinter light the day
that military turbo prop skidded in
at Toronto and everything unspooled
became a double take, soft focus
rolling *déjà vu*, home away from home
but nothing set to rights.
There were ravens in the frosted fields
and, given the ice, he knew he'd have to go.

He'd married her, my great aunt
in England. Rottingdean, south Sussex.
There were rivers, garlands, a castle
with a moat. A two week honeymoon
in Stratford, Oxford, Yorkshire
on the moors. A city girl she even loved
the cattle, their ripe milk scents, their ambling
down past coal sheds in the dawn.

He'd married her with his serviceman's ring –
Royal Norwegian Air Force. Gold lacquered scarlet
on gold. She wore it sixty years despite the men
who came and went, who smoked and danced and sang
but never matched his cut, his tone

the unpronounceable flavour of his skin
that carried notes of coral, hints of brine.

Here's what she left to me, DKT.
A room of books so rare
I must not let the light sift in.
A writing desk, initials upper left.
And in a rosewood box his ring
so I could give it you on the longest day of June
your passage booked, the airbus overheated
thrumming on the landing strip
its course already plotted
for New York, Tampa, Houston
all points west.

Trains at Tempe

Let me tell you about the trains, he said

How the moon won't bring you sleep
or the sun either, how it's all always
Peckinpah, Malick
on odd days pure Lynch
out there in Arizona

How they came each day at dawn
Santa Fe hot shots
Canadian Pacific freighters
all graffiti and gondolas, all lumber and grain
and makeshift crates of Asian figurines

How the earth on its axis stalled
while the low light fixed the camera
a full eight minutes and forty four seconds
and the film we are watching now
five thousand miles, three hundred and sixty six days later

unavoidably arrived
and the trains – unblessed, burdened – were again
gone

Allen Ginsberg's Bed

Hottest night in the history
of New York City, sweat slick electric
body stripped, spread eagled, solo
on Allen Ginsberg's bed
all the stars of the known universe
cascading through the hydrogen skull.

Allen Ginsberg is not at home.
Allen Ginsberg is a thousand miles away
in Boulder, Colorado conversing with Chogyam Trungpa.
I am a custodian, lone Vitruvian
man minding the premises merely.

Not thinking, just breathing
sucking air the way planes do
descending from unsayable altitudes
whole elaborate mechanism deliberately
getting used to surviving

midnight shell shock
punk up from behind back
mugging six blocks from
these windows, that door
this home a long way from home.

The gun, a Beretta, may or may not
have been metal, metaphysical.

Hey Allen Ginsberg I'm as unstrung as you were
mugged in that burned out basement
clutching poems, telephoning cops in the fluorescent bodega.

Wake up and here is Manhattan, an uncut
day for night sequence
film of a film
neither of us is able to edit
down to the final frame
to what it barely is.

Bob Dylan's Paintings

"Bob Dylan's paintings are not at all
what you'd expect of Bob Dylan.

They're watercolours washed with light
and a certain kind of effervescence,
the lot of them just coming down
with frivolity and gravitas
the two in equal measure."

You called that hot June night
from the Riverside to say
you'd been around the exhibition
not once but twice and might go back
again, if the schedule allowed.

You talked about the transport
and the pickup trucks, the sailing boats
observed from hotel balconies
the drifters and the diners
the disused beds and chairs
all of it a deckle edged dramatics
staged under claret skies.

"What's really knocked me sideways though
are these portraits of a woman in a pub
and a man up on a bridge.

There's four or five of both of them
the lines identical, give or take

but the colours and the tones
completely changed. The same thing
with a traintrack where it veers
westways into the middle distance.
Okay, they're variations on a theme
but there's something else besides…"

I wondered what he'd said to you, Bob Dylan,
that you didn't know before. Which story
about desire, desolation or being on the run
shook you to your boots each time you looked
and heard it play out differently?

The Map Is Not the Territory
after Alfred Korzybski

Somewhere in the middle distance
of a photograph shot down in Santa Fe, New Mexico
that familiar gesture floats, left hand signalling
from the rolled down driver's window
of a '68 cherry red Chevrolet Impala: *adios*.

It is impossible to see his face or catch
the music, salsa picked up from a border station.
The sun commits adultery, the soft top frays.
Still there are gleanings, a shower of mercury arrow
heads, the kind brought down Geronimo's prize pony

so desirous he to know death intimately.

At Medicine Lake

It is my birthday, or ought to be.
Lucky March, lightstruck the way snow is
when it arrives to cover itself
with a spring skin or deliver the volcanic Cascades

from first kingdoms to last.

Here is what you bring to me
two hands cupped around a lazurite bowl
tattooed ankles sifting through starched snake grass —
obsidian soul shard retrieved from the outer reaches

of the innermost house.

Angelino

By the side of a dark dream road…

—CORMAC MCCARTHY, *Suttree*

❧❧

Struck up home in the moted loft
of a barn out west of Proton township
forwhy no one can tell

Below dust devils and the children
of farmhands and horse handlers
drawing charcoal cartoons on the packed dirt road

You climb the sawtooth stairs
cotton muzzled ironing board, vintage 1942
under your arm, longnecked jar of sour mash
held aloft like torchflame

Your hair is black and mine
falls long, like sheaves you say
over and beyond your thief's shoulders

❧❧

High noon and the tide heading in.
Pensacola or New Orleans, it could be either,
violent gold light of the rimed Gulf Coast

My daughter without water wings
rescues your guitar, head and neck
and graceful rosewood body
dashed and riven in mooncobbled salts

We lay it on the sand and wait for you.
Quaver notes and minor chords
a ballad in three quarter time
picked out on the restless southern air

✥

Black on black: the boots, the hat
onyx ring a labyrinth
waistcoat, greatcoat, braided belt.
Still at a distance that glance
of turquoise at the throat

Up there on stage you make my name
an amulet, a cry cast like coinage to the stalls
dark somewhere I am banditted, holding out
the only known photograph of you
that winter when the city (call it Tallulah or Truckee)
fell at your feet in lightning strikes, histories

✥

On bleached lime spits I wear white
deerskin moccasins, guide an Appaloosa colt

the distance from our northerly encampment
to find a house I do not recognize
as yours, though you are stationed at the gable window
with astrolabe and telescope, a clutch of *mappae mundi*
discerning in its barbican and cupolae
the lines of galleons or gliders
while I ride on, the riverbed a red
and stricken maze beneath

એફ

Solarium, aquarium, planetarium?
It is March in Montreal
cold white light rebounding
off snowfields, jumpcuts
to bolts of anthracite and ebon

The place is glass domed, tropical
and voyeurwise I watch you
twinned, swimming
lengths in thermal waters where
the tattoos you wear are mine

એફ

Like anvils the thunderheads lord it over flattened crops.
The horizon comes up a backlit wound
stitched with neon sulphur. Singed scent of end days
drifts in at the Ford's wing window

We are driving east through torrents
low pressure troughs, traits of cyclone weather.
To the left the river, turgid, unseamed
to the right the mountain, stripped by scuds and squalls

I rehearse the route, border towns and prairie sideroads
the delta we've been aiming for
while you are sure this is another country altogether
its name about to show forth at the outskirts

in letters bold on uplit water towers
each one a sign and wonder
I'm unable or maybe just unwilling
to reckon through the blacktop's gravid glare

The Etymology of Animal

Who had the first word on dream flight?
What teleologies, what etiologies
do we declare adequate?

That lean shape hunted
to the Jack pine's stripped crown
could as easily be crow or cat
as your soul hiding out, scouring the tundra
for signs of groundswell, subterranean tremor
those sudden places where mine insists
on cartwheels, somersaults, banks and dives
making of flying an end in itself.

Deor, deuzon, animal me, animal you
living being which breathes
origins slip, elide while we
pitch tupiks on pingos
safety and risk, causes and effects
have abandoned to circumstance.

Totem Dreams

White Horse

This mare is airborne!
Outback creature, albino galleon
scudding the cauldron desert
her weight judders under me
mounts Uluru, hooves chipping
the red rock rim
she overshoots, leaps, makes my mouth
a jubilant delta sluicing oblivion.

Green Snake

Wednesday's *Guardian* blacks my hands.
Set in kanji its headlines talk
of Hermes and his caduceus.
Out of origami newsprint folds
a tight jawed emerald opheodrys
strikes the meaty ounce of flesh
hammocking thumb and index finger.
No scarlet pain jag, just
a note tapped fast in neon nerve text:
This is not coincidence.
Torsive it mimics

my wounded scoliotic spine
luminescent good luck charm
ferrying the antidote of antidotes.

Red Otter

The manor house is Ontario gothic,
russet towers in a maple wood.
Spirited skyward my daughter and I
are hostage to the cantilevered attic
kneelers at its gable window, steep
gallows drop to the river below.
She spies the first – *lutra, otor* –
lithe, joyous, cornelian tattoo
surfing the fluvial current
guiding playstruck kin upstream
to sand spits, lake lands.
The crocodiles thresh and raddle:
harvesters, lynch mob
they stain the estuary
a crimson hinterland.

Burying the Raven

Let him come back to me whole, in dreams stain
my bleached mornings, undead familiar.

Let his sable wingspan outgleam itself
in death, the swarming mites turn to snow.

Let his scimitar beak inscribe on my emerging
skull the poetry of the stratosphere.

Let his brave talons transport
my long shanks, my folded ribs, my irreducible heart

to the tops of cedars where under
Pacific cloud cover he places in my mouth

the almandine blessing stone
I have set into his.

Ottersong

This is where the wolf crosses over
where owls skim the night's meniscus

and feral red deer
graze in blanched ruins.

We enter the water where the stone road
leaves the woods.

We enter the water, acquire the skins of otters.
Burdened with songs and incantations

our river blood, our sea flesh
favour your heart and carry it under the world.

Death's red stars hang mute. Lit up by their own
code of violence they stop your breath.

What gathers inside that season's gap
has the flavour of sacrament at starvation's close.

Killed, you split the surface and the ocean
is rainshards of malachite and jacinth.

Your heart beats scarlet, scarlet.
Everywhere there is air.

Here is what it means to be a sack of shells.
Here is what it means to be holy.

I take off my skin and you are restored to life.

Flight

By habit I would hunt and delve
worry the meaning of dreams about flight
not in biplanes or bombers or featherweight gliders
but solo, body neither machine nor animal
nor sheer soul either
rather a candent rain of molecules
oxidized, dextrous, wired, designed
for tracking roofbeams, skimming floorboards
grazing the tarmac, rushing
that porthole southwest of Arcturus
its lure, its thrown uncanny music.

Until you cautioned not to speculate
instead to take the thing whole
(a gold stone, a cuneiform tablet)
be sated knowing that movement
is all the property we own.

This weather the nights are short
and laminar the light rides in
on bright neap tides.
I trace its long retreat, the lough's span
and west out over the plateau
sometimes with you
but mostly I fly alone.

III

The Creation of Man

after Chagall

In Chagall's painting of the angel
ferrying the fallen skyward
the sun is a whirligig and behind the moon

a god reads to human choirs
a story of peace
from the yellow canvas of conviction.

Amongst the bricabrac
(peacock, donkey, flying fish
dwarf priest's ladder, his teetering menorah)

the painter's signature – two lovers drowning
in Carpathians of blue, the embryonic whisper
of an infant child held up, looking glass between them.

In this corner of the frame
the damages of history
cached in palimpsest.

Sleeping in Your Mother's House

What is the name of those blossoms, pink starbursts on stilts
protecting like samurai the limits of her garden?
Your mother declares them the national flower of Japan.
Sent to scythe the luscious stalks I read their signature—
cuneiform rows of exclamation marks.

Head resting on rolled bamboo I am listening out
for my daughter's long jumps into *aphrodisiac* and *insomnia*
the juggernaut *hypnosis*, daydreaming of Kyoto
where a woman dressed in saffron and sorrel
descends a train, footfall on quadrants of raked pebbles.

To sleep at midday within speaking distance
of eucalyptus and magnolia, to court again your father's ghost
weeping under the felled sakura and hear in the singular
pulse of your breath (slight yet insistent as snowfall)
the plenitude of rivers in spate, the rise of green lakes

is to be nowhere and eastward, at once
the bleak warrior dedicated to seppuku
and the lapsed defiant October slipstream neither kite
nor kittiwake nor long tailed jaeger can survive.
Such typhoons this house has weathered!

Your mother stands, her ninety retainers at ease
handfeeds the elusive ouzel, the shy merlin
from her bottomless satchel of seeds.

Enter Tezcatlipoca

This is the pool of silence, it has no shores.
Its tributaries run inward, cryptic and cold.
We live where the city doubles back
on itself, devours demons and guardians.
At table your hands build temples inside coffee smoke.
Rage nests in my lap, it has an obsidian beak
and the wolf made of bone, convoluted pendant
on a leather thong, leaps.

Tezca, south of the border man, offers a juniper box
spills out its contents, fifty two numbered pieces.
I follow him downstairs to the galley, where the kitchens are.
You keep your place by the window, snow insulating
the double panes. There is something to be said but
it is nothing he doesn't already know.

Virtual

Not so long ago you told me
it means something close to almost
but not yet quite entirely or, more exactly,
in effect but not in fact. Which is to say
the ochre tempo of your voice
your exclusive range of scent
that way you have of straddling kitchen chairs
all exist elsewhere.

But then again I have your moving image
and your words, or at least the shapes
you chose to make of them, the dramas they perform
while you yourself are in the wings
behind the camera, tuning off-pitch strings
or, if it's early in the day, observing Catalina
after love idly brush her hair.

No More Knives

The top drawer bristles
with rows of forks and skewers
ridged and slope backed carvers.
Off to the left a host
of paring, dicing
boning knives, cleavers.

Even the double handled blade
that once upon a time entered
so unceremoniously
a four tiered wedding cake.

Whose dream kitchen was this
the west window exposing
scoured rockface, the east
the blitzed out heart
of the enduring city?

Who designed the seriously vibrant
atrium, such dramatic domestic interiors?
His name is here, inscribed on my
vitreous rib bridge, like hers is there
cut into the thick of your sternum.

No one lays claim
to pain like yourself.
Yours is the royal red

knit round the core of August peach flesh
the flare and flash
of gutted pomegranate.

My own is deep cyan
the rinsed throb of ice coombs or
my recklessly high threshold
for delirium and crash.

In syllabics you speak to me
freebooting messenger
with a black nightingale
offer your weathered wrists
their serried landscapes

as I surrender my pirate's horde
of assegais and kukri
their notched hafts, their scored tips
to our kindred oath.

Leaving Azure for Jasper

i.

Canoes outrigged for long distance voyaging
the first ones bequeathed us

drumsong, throat chant
their islands incanting *nothing dies*

not musk ox, not moccasin
not beluga, not kookaburra

revealing how shapes shift and all souls
are marked out, yoked

on the carbon highway, bleeding stars
and their light into precambrian landscapes.

This story has no beginning, it is part of the way
water moves into land and lays claim, its words

emerge from deep places, aboriginal
souterrains, continents adrift and nameless.

ii.

Opaque jet, my blood was ever my own.
Unstilled the heart's rhythm came to believe
in others, a reciprocity of lifelines.

Who opened the stained window
that February morning, the meridian
releasing cascades of azure?

What fire transfigured my bones
when gowned in leaf and madder
I understood the necessity of sacrifice?

What celestite invocation called forth
out of bleak March rains this child
whose gemstones are jade and amethyst?

Three times I died and three times
was brought back up out from under
chthonian rivercourse to light.

In seasons of willow and holly I tilled
hewed rock gardens at the sea's limit
while my daughter made communion with fresh water.

iii.

Betrayal is the universe confined
in a steel jawed box, panopticon of pain

walled in grief. In a summer of sorrows
under the eclipse of the sun

at equinox, in a night of knives
the endurance of loss.

Blade or card, justice conceals its actual shape
it wears the shades of symmetry.

Cast out to valleys where thunder dogs
the wicked and the clean

logical moons confound the simple
songlines laid in faith.

No language avails. I speak and undisguised
my figure cuts umbrae in dust.

iv.

Suffering is carmine, it tastes of iron.
It settles under the tongue
nascent creature, earthed in probability.
It tears down dominions
replenishes hinterlands
nourishes.

Ungeminied I
idle on the vacant doorstep
between one world and another
inhale the jasper atmosphere of shift
become jackal, ocelot, blackbuck
zendik adept in the ethics of animals
at rest in the kingdom of my own bones.

Caz

I dreamed a man whose name was Caz
he spoke in fluent Quechua and his eyes
were lined with midnight kohl.
He'd come, he said, to ease the pain
of something lost or just about to be.

I made poems for him and followed
when he led the way down passages
thick with lime and jacaranda, the clockwork
inner sanctum of a city built by Incan alchemists.

There were stairs and then a doorway
where he knelt and brewed white tea
and when I asked the question he'd expected
he said his name was Cave, or maybe Calve.

He wasn't you or me exactly, though
his shoulders held the imprint of an angle
either one of us could carry off
when saddled up and riding.

And just before he left, an ovoid agate
balanced like a green bird on his palm
he spoke of birthing rituals, a strategy
to transmute grief into the look of love.

Feathers

He shared my father's birthday
twenty-fifth day of the cruellest month.

Iranian political refugee
he'd just turned twenty three

live wire wide awake in the green
dream of that first English spring

his mother weightless without her hijab
navigating the maze of Camden Market

his father sorrowful and estranged, heart
surgeon learning to pilot a London cab.

Afloat he celebrated, jiving, raving
in masks made out of feathers

embroidered kaftans, horned headdresses
outlandish spikes and studs.

Lodestar, the fashionistas coveted
his sense of style

adopted face paint, Persian slippers
wardrobes thronged with one-off hats and scarves

while the Queensway kids invented rap-ghazals
and googled Mohsen Namjoo

Tehran's homegrown Bob Dylan
approved the music's bold collapse of east and west.

Mornings he played backgammon
(Babylonian tic-tac-toe)

beside the slackbacked Serpentine
and from the temple perched atop

the ziggurat of his laughter
lamentation thousandfold

for that mute howl of voices
proscribed, obliterated

the incremental clause embedded
in his riff on the root of consanguinity.

Ease

It is the season of Aquarius
the water bearer.
From the driver's seat you tell me
the gone day tasted of spring
its scents condensed into stars
and the shipyard's lights
collaring the rugged horizon.

The car's an automatic, it glides.
Silent my daughter thumbs
the pebble smoothness as we
mount the rise and coast
out onto the shoreline highway.

What I notice is not
the illuminated dash or the odometer
clocking over ninety thousand
but the structure of your hands.
They are the hands of fishermen.
Watching them I believe we are in Canada
heading north to Haida Gwaii.

Lightning, you claim, is the embodiment
of coincidence, good fortune the direct result
of courtesy and timing. Like distance
not an obstacle if the engine is primed.

Slick night drive, nineteen pounds sterling
in bills and change. That tailored oilskin
carries ground water and clay.
Teal, it has the same shades as your voice

timbre I'll recall for an uncertain
number of days after you drive away
balancing two brimful buckets
of rain and glancing
in the rear view mirror to see
with what ache or ease
I carry mine.

Bone Tattoo

Soporific that is your voice
the only drug pure enough
to wake me, shift the deep
Sargasso settled and resettled
in the basin of my heart.

Words decorate air
in your absence, the hall
becomes a cloister with one
three light window, nave
where I eat each slanted syllable

and keep my own accents.
Tightened like the lid of a drum
Saskatchewan prairie is chrome
yellow and white, a different sea or
our *sui generis* chapel

where nothing is discarded. The daily poems,
the urgent prayers, all last minute utterings
are cadence rendered serif and intaglio
on the bonescript of tibia and fibula
of femur, radius, ulna.

Ancient Twins

Wintering by the Sea of Cortez
azure swells break on my doorstep

deliver a memory of rift, or the idea of riders
limbering up for the next ride south.

Seductive as Baja afternoons
citrus weather, red ocotillo bloom

pacific water harbours a grieving heart
only strawberry moons know how to comfort.

If death is a clapboard junction, a quasar
or a cedar chest of ground gypsum

is neither here nor there. My hair drips salt
and my feet are joyous, setting out

for unmapped deserts, the corded chapparal
where my cinnamon twin gathers

his bundle of spilled amulets
(onyx beads, diced roots, pinto corn)

knows in his migrant bones this crossing
takes both our names for its syllabary.

Lemniscate

It was after the tornado, the one
razed our walnut trees to kindling,
that you brought me out to Calaveras County
its hills and heat charged valleys
dominoed with tombstones.

We sat our horses, two raw pintos,
in the shadow of a farmer's
makeshift ossuary.
The death's head on the lintel
wore wapiti antlers.

Inside your wrist a figure eight
tattooed and on my tongue you placed
a word I could scarce pronounce
but understood it signified
the crush of sand weighed down my saddle bags.

That was just before the light
washed from sepia to bleach
and I drank the canteen dry
and you, *peregrino curandero*, rode on.

What Gold We Gather

On the periphery there is gunfire, a seam of reprisals.
We meet at the heart of a forest where my poems
are a listening to animals, your acts and scenes
a conversation in voices striated with zeal and underhand.

I am staking tents, small outposts
on traplines where the climate is murderous
while you construct cathedrals, their kaleidescope windows
letting in just the right amount of brokenness.

These are our ways of saying everything that escapes—
floating blueprints, an architecture of invisibility.
Open your mouth and a gold sunstone, oblation brought down
from pain's tower, ascends. A lark, or the first word
                                                    in a new language.

My You

Morning is a thicket of sibilants
it offends mine ear.

Shadowplay on sheers.
The attendants attend
water bearers, alms givers
alles vorsichtig, all
utterly other.

Against their hammered
fricatives and plosives
I have erected a labial forest
slippery gullygrove
sans ingress or egress.

Queen chambered at its green core
I defy the noonday sun
to cleave, unleave me
of excess, lay bare the ormolu
vowel of the terminal desert.

Sudden as snow the doorway
rustles. Wings. Vaulting or settling?

Tongue cannot tell but glides, elides
tries

my...

        my...

                my...

you!

Such thunderous, luxuriant applause:
the mother seeking son ocean
crescendos at our feet.

Kilrea in Gemini

I'd call but she'd be gone to local service
a funeral or a christening, or have driven down the line
attending to sick neighbours with stews and casseroles
to speed their healing fast along.

Come winter she'd go tracking deer to measure
her hand's span against their prints
or hike across the Sperrins just to catch
an unexpected sighting of Judas in the pines.

She knew the names of comets and the zodiac's design
had memorized taxonomies and could recount biographies
of South Sea island travellers, lady tourists
who a century before she'd learned to split the surface

of the shallows where that stripe of skerries
nestles north of White Park Bay
had navigated jungle heats and coral reefs
in the ruby throes of far flung Vanuatu.

She had a twin who came round once or twice a season
with a Jew's harp and odd artefacts from Egypt
he had horses and she'd match him at flat racing
out there between the headlands and the sea.

I called to her that time the rains came heavy
but there was nothing, just the beat of surf
all tangled up inside those russet high notes
her gemshorn ocarina used to send.

Torr Head

In the middle distance
a sheep
among sheep
reclining on shredded outcrops
resembles nothing
so much as your father's
favourite easy chair.

You swear its soul's
been hung out to dry
metaphysical scarecrow
guldering obscenities
down Atlantic seabreeze.

We've grown used
to your second sightings
but sometimes I wonder
why even the long lens
fails to pick out
the wolverines
the snowy owls
and now this sheep
(who reminds me of nothing
so much as Murakami's
wild one)

while you tune in
to the coast guards
telegraphing west
by northwest
conversing
with Windigo
and his cache
of new found land
sheep.

The Elephants in Ann Street

Climbing down is out of the question.
We are here to stay. Wedded, incontrovertible
twinned it's said, but wrongly.
One glares, the other winks.

Blue ghosts and grey ghosts salute us.
Loyal to the fickle wash of passersby
we are as close as they will ever come
to totems. This is the middle circle of lost familiars.

Under our nouveau auspices the city's last
builder of ships, moon in his surplus rucksack
tunes in the bluesman sailing Pottinger's Entry
quizzes the façade's unsung circus march—

> Who made the elephants in Ann Street?
> Not Mackintosh, not MacNair, but a woman
> graceless hands in love with the geometry
> of the animals of the Indian subcontinent.

Drinking Mojitos with Ali in
the Japanese Restaurant in Belfast

"The oldest people on earth live
on the islands of Okinawa,
a diet of fish and vegetables."

Over the sashimi and wasabi
those mint green eyes defy
any one of them to outdo you

when it comes to sheer
overdetermined
endurance of the odds.

Obsequious, courteous, the waiter tells us
the second carafe of saki
is on the house, that he was born

in a ger in Khovd Province in 1962
but as luck or loss would have it
came of age on the sidestreets of Havana.

"Longevity," you say, "is never more
than a question of which story
we elect to tell, how elaborate the digressions

or if it's visuals are wanted
which filter's set to cut the glare
of winter light on glass."

You smile and he smiles too
at something nearly missed
but squarely understood

our Cuban Mongolian dinner guest
who bowing shoeless sets about
casting breadcrumbs to the carp

until the conversation's run its course
and you're ready to head out
sharp skiff at full tilt skimming

the lubricious rim
of this or that
amaranthine archipelago.

Big Yellow Boots

She was lame at tracking
would mistake
wolverine for lynx
muskrat for raccoon.
One time her own footprints
for her brother's.

I should know.
I'm her father.
My father set the region's
slyest traplines
snared creatures even the Cree
couldn't find names for.

The day we got Lu Lu
it was too cold to snow.
Called her after those
crazy divers, *oiseaux fous*
her head half away
with him in the moon.

Until that one from
north of the north
from Wolf Hill
no long black coat but
big yellow boots
instead.

Heavy on the gas
he'd graze the brake
for amusement.
Speed demon
with a collection of stripes.
And when he ran
antelope.

He skinned things
sometimes alive.
The moon eclipsed
itself where he walked
(three bears barely
touching down)
backwards across the fresh snow
of her heart.

Big yellow boots
smooth soles well worn in.

She hunts now.
Bigger game than any of us
ever knew in these parts.

Waiting for Snow

i

For three days we listened to weather reports
unseasoned diviners scrying entrails or
casting lots under the flight paths of birds.
It was ancient crouching by fires like that
holding cedar splints to gauge the Siberian wind's force.
When the snow fell you were on the plateau.
Here by the sea it lay one night only
the ceremony over by daybreak.

ii

Third time this week I dream of the desert.
Not just any desert, the Mojave Desert.
Out of it walks a white dog that is not a coyote.
I load it into a pickup truck and drive it home
to my daughter who names it Snow.

Jackalope High

What is there to be sure of, out here under Cassiopeia's
overturned wagon, the palaeozoic darkness dazzling
the infrared eyes of every animal within range?

Two hours before dawn each sound has its ghost
arroyos awash with echoes retreating
the way brittle bone goes grindingly to ash.

This is no wasteland but the ethics of justice.
Certainty's vista – a raddled stone, a grafted limb.
The desert is in love with fissures, fractures, intimate mutations.

O my hybrid *companero*, half warrior, half corsair
in spaces blank as these we taught ourselves to hunt
by gut instinct alone, bring down quarry in velvet silence.

More fleet than spilt mercury we divided
the spoils and ate, never guessing
one another's actual names, or how easy it might be

to undo the miracle that keeps
the jackalope, the thunderbeast
      lightwrapped
            riddled with belief
                  a sure forty paces out in front.

The House with One Hundred Rooms

Not even houses built in the dreams of wayfarers
have so many rooms as this one.
Each is a different colour.
Chinese boxes, they open and close
on one another like paper lanterns
or a jigsaw of souterrains.
Escher staircases give way
to ruined turrets, and in the cellars
a carnival of frayed sofas
collapses under the weight of possible conversations.

No matter that the plaster
shatters into a fretwork of broken trails
or that the paint unleaves, ruby and copper snakeskin.
My hands are intent on restoring
every fracture, all the fallen beams.
Outside it is Canada
frozen lakes and charcoal blue treelines.
There will be twelve seasons
before the snow geese come back
and I can place a purple
Amazonian orchid just beyond the reach
of that moonstruck great bay window.

IV

Threshold

Air gives what is indispensable to live, to grow and to speak — to each one, man or woman, and to a relation between two not dominated by the one or by the other.

—LUCE IRIGARAY, *The Way of Love*

At summits, in the mouths of caves
here are the rooms we choose for home
their fabric the lineaments of a radical winter
scapes with neither doors nor windows
more transient than tents, open to stars
sidereal nocturnes their shifting coordinates.

Avid for air, the threshold's gleam
we speak our same and singular tongues:
I become the occult oryx
while your bones grow a carbon forest
where I lose you, win, lose again
wake in you poems, their rhythms
the marquetry of a fifth season
or the cries of ancient murrelets
coasting the atoll's shorn rim.

Density/Distance

Richard is telling of swimming
with sea turtles off Kauai
(their shy, playful gestures
the ocean's alien clarity)

when they settle, a blizzard
in ash and snow
smelling of Hopedale, Heart's Content
unsalvageable homelands to the west.

These are Canada's wild, lost geese.
Twenty six, and the day St Stephen's.
Do we construe them as an omen or
agree a breach in the aerodynamics?

Too cold for cameras we note
the sun's wide angled incision
into the shipyard's rent heart

mention sea salt, desert sand
the physics of corrosion
the metaphysics of transmigration.

Tench

Nothing holds body and soul
together on the ridgebacked
height of June (sun scaling
vermilion zeniths)
like the long antiphonal draw
succour, solace, balm, boon.
Water is the original
song of songs.

Luciferous zero
it tastes of sweetgrass
the stalk's tender core.
It tastes mineral — salt hints
mica notes, an undertone of iron.
Spring fed source in Oxfordshire
a disused gravel pit
where bronze humped tench idle
stunned, intoxicate
suspended yet animate
barbels alert to every
shot of energy.
So plentiful this year
you could lift them with your hands.

I watch you summon them
— *tinca, tinca* —
earth man's honest body

Herculean under the weight
of worlds I've sidestepped
up to this day when
no longer at home in Church Road
you come like the lions
did at nightfall to my doorstep
that season in the Transvaal
to claim one single
glass of water.

Hollow Bone

The rainy season came between one encounter
and the next. Coy at the fulcrum
an opal moon, eclipsed plenitude a trace

of your two rings (one a gift from Oaxaca
the other stolen in the highlands of Peru)
their run on inscription I could read

with my eyes closed—
Love in the present tense
is no love at all.

It was under that selfsame moon
or so it seemed
you drew music from the hollow

bone of a jungle bird
(wing of quetzal
rib of macaw)

then declined to speak
of anything but mountains or
the echo bound pyramid at Kukulan

that bleached flute, its stops and gaps
having put an end to all
but the most seasoned morphic resonance.

Seven Poems after Frida Kahlo

They Ask for Planes and Only Get Straw Wings

Who is it says I am not equipped to fly?
Who has lassoed my skirts with twine
and nailed my feet to the floor?
Who dared tether with wires my wings
rooted them to invisible rafters
a mercy hole no one can see?
Who determines me *chingada*
the wounded one, the torn open, the deceived?

Not-I, Not-I
screech the monkeys, weep the deer.

No Tehuana angel I choose to pilot my plane
(a replica bomber, gift from the wide world to me)
out over the edge of the ocean.
Here, give me a pencil, a brush.
Where in grey plumes it plummets I soar
into some god's gaping jaws, you will see.

The Flying Bed

Could you have been there
would you have brought
a single purple orchid
its petals lustrous and full blown
unscented as your skin before love
the same flower Diego
is said to have given Frida
that sad summer in Detroit?

On the banks of rouge rivers
whose shoulders are prairies
bearing at distant rims
the iron clad look of industry
we give birth to death
his club foot, his moon skull
his coiled, wicked laughter
that collapses sheet metal around us
where tuned to a flamenco
choreography shot through with pain
bright as Coyoacán skies
we gather and begin again.

Beyond plain counting the numbers
of our lost children. Their possible
selves dissolve in ether nets
the flying bed I've washed up on
hands full of red ribbons leashed

to six balloons tricked out
in images of wealth and poverty
of longing and its counterpart.

I'll hold them until you return
(snails concealed in waistcoat pockets)
from coastal waters where wild
the white horses, *mesteños*, run and run.

The Mask

Even the cactus sheds its tears.

What do you imagine I am hiding
behind this Malinche false face?

Are you certain I am there at all?
Is this a self-portait
or not?

The tourists will come and go
remarking the papier-mâché's
punk tuft of purple hair
the carp's mouth
the flushed traitor's cheeks.

They will avoid the eyes
entirely, noting instead the ring
how it seems to contain
fields of rain.

They will say the mask is camouflage
a trick cloaking betrayal, humiliation
and love, an overabundance of it.

That beneath the mother
of Mexico's exquisite grief

I remain the inscrutable Aztec queen
I was born to be.

And they would not be wrong.

But *mi hermana* here's the detail
La Gran Ocultadura could not conceal—
the eyes, the ones somewhere inside
the penknifed holes-for-eyes,
belong to jungle creatures
for whom weeping is no option.

The Wounded Deer

Nine trees in the dead wood
nine tines on my antlered head
and some would say alchemically
nine points of entry, arrowshafts at sharp
right angles to my polished velveteen
flint heads daubed, perchance, in albified curare.
Not a bow in sight.
But at a distance water, always water
piscean, aquamarine and there above it lightning
June skies threaded with red gold veins.

Suspended I clear the windtorn branch
beneath my hooves, its living leaves.
Apparitions each to burn the seal on fortune or ill fame.
Ferine, carnival, we go tricked out in hope
gambolling, galloping, striking a good pace
drinking in the dry *cañada*'s crystal air
the desert's bold astronomy, its music of the spheres
to flatlands where we fall for death's sleek isomer
high cheekbones, flowstone gait, jewelled teeth aglitter
take up the palette he so courteously lays down
hematite and malachite, cinnabar, quicksilver
those delicate earth tones, those clear cut hues and cries.

Thinking about Death

Her gaze extinguishes everything in sight
this woman who resembles Nefertiti,
all wild intelligence harnessed
to lashings of imperturbable beauty.

O god I will make her again my double
her husband's sly collaborator
poised up there with her head
in the leaves of life, the thorns of death.

I watch her watching me watch her
give birth to herself. Contraries, midwives
white Huitzilopochtli, black Tezcatlipoca
are quick to notice her prominent brow

adorned with its miniature memento mori
skull and crossed bones a cameo *cavalera*
one more self portrait singing
out on the desert's shore a roundelay

about a woman, the earth's own mother
who, keeping an eye on both of us
makes it her lot to give and take
with the same hand.

The Dream

What is the name of my actual lover?
In truth it is neither Nikolas nor Julien
nor even Diego. Rather I court
the star attraction himself, *La Muerte*.

A joke to keep the town guessing or a token
to remind myself alone how day by day
he inhabits my bones, his marked time
spent making my skeleton his own

I give my favourite traitor, sweet
life size Easter puppet, pride of place
his lank thighs reclining
atop the canopy of my four poster bed.

No one knows me half so intimately as he does.
When I paint the pair of us the bed flies
and we are adrift, released into floating worlds
cloudscapes of the *pedregal* for backdrop.

I am asleep but he is wide awake and grinning
rigged out with a network of explosives, left hand
bearing a trim bouquet of lavenders and pinks
coy Judas to my dreaming Malinche

who under blankets gold as suns
considers the conditions of the afterlife
as his spilled entrails, *tripa de Judas*
take root and cover me in the foliage of deceit.

Roots

Reclining on Wolf Hill in my orange dress
and my black *zapatillas* no one notices
these highland vistas could be cloud or scrub
or even an apothecary's terraced herbarium
(archaic antidotes to a myriad of freak ailments)
whole bleached and broken scape the floating
alembic where my body finds itself adrift
levitated chest and midriff, clavicle to viscera
cut away, stark hiatus, frameless lacuna
cleansed rectangular revelation of a window
wide open to the climate, the climbing stalks and vines
which coming into leaf weep bloods
as much of my own making as the osculant earth's.

Across the river's mouth your house
quivers radiant in spent heat, omphalic
point of departure, its geometry the primal constellation.
Through telescopes you will pick out
on my plateau one lick of flame, unquenchable
as your own heart struck through and through
by corms and rhizomes, mute stigmata of fidelity
to the settlement's weird algebra
or some synaptic source.

Un Hombre del Camino

And then there was that winter when we met.
He drove a white Cordoba, its contours barely there
inside the highway's iced up corridors
a crystal ship, a car finagled for free from strangers
to make the drive due north, catch the tail end
of a February thaw and watch the bay break up.
To photograph the disused yards, the trains
the clapped out Shur Gain elevators designed
for housing crops the farms had ceased to sow.
To get an angle on that bypassed midwest town
I'd left behind seven hard won years ago.

The fields were full of shapes he'd never come across before –
illuminated silos rimed with hoar, in flailing rows
the county's first display of wind turbines, electric shocks
along a dim potato rise, the holy shows of scriptures
hoisted high on windwarped barnboard sidings.
At night the motel rooms tuned to the swank blues talk
of strung out gibbous moons that came and went like inland tides

while he would make things up – ballads, refrains, choruses
that told of how the whole place came to be.
There was a Fender, or maybe a bespoke Gibson
it gets harder to remember, and every shot he took
he named it with a number then a phrase
set down in songbooks, the kind the village pharmacist
reserved for backroom crannies kept under lock and key.

He might have come from Texas or Cholula
spoke no Spanish, but could call up after dark
odd smatterings of border rhyme.
Said he liked the place I'd brought him to, it gave him something
nowhere else had done, some medicine, some antidote
or the inkling of a really first class line.

Once upon a time in Juarez or deeper
into Mexico there was a man and built inside of him
a box, a treasured chest, and in the box a road
the colour and the texture of graphite or thrashed flint.
That road scored scrimshaw into skin and bone and still he drove it.
I was there. I know. I somehow stayed to tell.

La Casa del Anhelo

Across the lagoon his house stands bone bright white
intricate invention of an odd northerly zonda

its windfashioned turrets, its wrought iron balconies
magnified by water invisible in the slung desert air.

Camped on scoured beaches his *cazadores* claim it
espejismo, say those who sight it are granted *milagros*.

Extinguished the sun ignites salt brush, soapweed,
the abandoned *aldea*, its madstone walls in flames.

They depart, the hunters, gathering greyhounds and rifles
alert to every twist and halt in this *corrido*

given me these twenty years, its skeined lines drawn
from the adamantine where wolves do their whispering

and bats their beryl chatter, unguarded ground
where I lived coming and going with the animals

or the sea fed lake itself, like him a creature
hallowed and admonished, though he knew it not.

Sueño del Padre

There were lightning strikes that Sunday you drove south
to make a movie or to star in one, I can't remember which.
Across your wake gale winds rode in disguised as twisters
their violence tore our passion vines right up by the roots.

That was the night your father chose to visit
we met at home in his oak study by the sea
or maybe it was in an attic chamber
gold light refracting cubes and trapezoids

on books books books, geometries of them
and letters written while the war was on
something about a camel and a cargo plane
crash landed out on salt flats at the Cape

a woman he loved whose name the desert gods
inscribed into the quadrants of an ailing heart
and how he'd sometimes see you
dressed in black from head to heel

same way I was seeing him, at a distance
and departing, your gait but not your voice
his border intonations cut adrift and gliding
from this scene to the setup for the next.

The Sun on His Back

In my daughter's atlas
Spain is the colour of a cool satsuma
the one I watched him peel and section
not so long ago, fingers recollecting
the contours of a dozen Christmas mornings.

And even if he'd chosen not to name
the places and the dates
(each one a mystery, each one an abstract noun)
before he had to go
I would know the sun crossing
the skin plateau my pelvis makes
is the same sun casting
blessings on his back where he works
measuring light and the angle
of the Andalusian mountain's influence.

Today's the seventh day of March.
I trace the lines from there to here
distracted midway by the centre fold
to wondering if desire like the double helix
(those symmetrical economies)
has something yet to say about the way
fresh water finds a second life far underground
or sea creatures routes to sanctuary
without recourse to maps.

Tattoo Land

With sheaves of feathers in our arms
we go down at nightfall under a copper moon
to unlock the sea gate and be where the water is
prepare cypress boats painted cochineal, indigo.

Here there are gypsies, vagabonds, pilgrims. High astride
the horizon leopard and lizard, the south's constellations.
Lost to plainspeaking we tend the tide's fires
make of salt or zinc alphabets a curing ceremony.

The journey happens. Not a word said.
In such light my bones become you
our markings identical their colours inverse

our wilderness hearts confused in their travelling.
This way the ship, its open wings, its living cargo
flies and makes landfall, sole at the sky's margin.

Acknowledgements

For reading and responding to draft versions of these poems I would like to thank Ronnie Bailie, Alison Crawford and Clare McCotter. Deepest gratitude to Seán Virgo, whose editorial acumen and generosity of spirit remain unrivalled.

Special gracias to Sky, for listening to all the stories.

I am indebted to the Ontario Arts Council for providing me with a Writers' Reserve Grant which enabled the completion of this collection.

"Snow Tea" has been published previously in *Exile: The Literary Quarterly*.